SELF-COMPASSION

LEARN TO LOVE YOURSELF

FOR WHO YOU ARE.

Kristin Carmichael & Kyle Neff.

Copyright 2018 by Kristin Carmichael & Kyle Neff - All rights reserved.

The following eBook is reproduced below with the goal of providing information that is as accurate and reliable as possible. Regardless, purchasing this eBook can be seen as consent to the fact that both the publisher and the author of this book are in no way experts on the topics discussed within and that any recommendations or suggestions that are made herein are for entertainment purposes only. Professionals should be consulted as needed prior to undertaking any of the action endorsed herein.

This declaration is deemed fair and valid by both the American Bar Association and the Committee of Publishers Association and is legally binding throughout the United States.

Furthermore, the transmission, duplication or reproduction of any of the following work including specific information will be considered an illegal act irrespective of if it is done electronically or in print. This extends to creating a secondary or tertiary copy of the work or a recorded copy and is only allowed with express written consent from the Publisher. All additional right reserved.

The information in the following pages is broadly considered to be a truthful and accurate account of facts and as such any inattention, use or misuse of the information in question by the reader will render any resulting actions solely under their purview. There are no scenarios in which the publisher or the original author of this work can be in any fashion deemed liable for any hardship or damages that may befall them after undertaking information described herein.

Additionally, the information in the following pages is intended only for informational purposes and should thus be thought of as universal. As befitting its nature, it is presented without assurance regarding its prolonged validity or interim quality. Trademarks that are mentioned are done without written consent and can in no way be considered an endorsement from the trademark holder.

Contents

What Is Self-Compassion 1

Why You Might lack Self-Compassion 7

Mindful Self-Compassion 12

    How Mindfulness Helps You Build Self-Love ... 12

    1: Know what you think, feel, and want most times 13

    2: Separate your positive thoughts and opinions from the negative ones 14

    3: Train yourself to become more mindful of what goes on around you 14

    Practice Mindful Breathing 15

    Develop a Mantra 15

    Be mindful of everything else 16

    Practice Self-Respect 17

    1: Carry yourself with dignity 17

    2: Present yourself in the most respectable way 18

    3: Have a high opinion of yourself 18

Knowing Yourself 20

1: Weigh your strengths against your weaknesses 21

2: Accept your shortcomings and commit to overcoming them 21

3: Acknowledge your strengths and build upon them... 22

4: Convince yourself you have all you need to live a great life 22

Developing Self-Compassion 24

Social Anxiety Disorder:...................................... 24

Academic Procrastination 25

Increase in Depression.. 26

Lack of Gratitude:.. 27

Feeling Rushed 27

Distraction 28

Rejection Sensitivity.. 28

Dealing with Emotions 34

How To Deal With Resentment Destroyin Relationships.. 36

The Contracts We Make In Our Heads 37

How We Talk To Ourselves................................... 40

Self-Acceptance Exercise 42

- Self-Forgiveness 44
- Building Unshakable Self-Esteem 46

The Power of Self-Compassion 49

Overcome Your Past 70
- Turning weaknesses into strengths 70
- Accept your weaknesses 71
- Get good enough at them 71
- Hire your weaknesses 72
- Accept your failures 72
- Let failure free you 79
- Learn from them 79
- Make Plan B's and C's 80
- Accept that certain things are not good for you. 80
- Take responsibility for your life 81
- Embrace the pain 81

Physiology of Self-Compassion 83
- What is a positive mind? 93
- The two wolves within 93
- Conditioned minds 94
- The power of the subconscious mind 95
- The Way to a Positive Mindset 102

Practice Affirmations 103

Practice Gratitude 104

Surround yourself with positive people 105

Be aware of your thoughts 106

See the positive in everything 107

Spread positivity around 107

No more surviving, it's time for thriving! 109

Forgive others 110

Putting Yourself Into Action 112

1: Never miss your night sleep for anything 112

2: Engage in physical exercises 113

3: Mind what you eat 114

Occasionally pamper yourself 114

When you do well, reward yourself 115

Simplify your life 116

Review your circle of friends 117

Review your To-Do list 118

Become a Minimalist 119

Self-Compassion & Relationships 119

Maintaining Self Compassion 123

Memorizing Compassionate Phrases 125

Self-compassion Diary 126

Morning Rituals 127

Practice Acts of Kindness 127

Self-compassion through Writing 128

Conclusion 131

Go places you have always avoided 132

Take up challenging tasks 133

Chapter 1

WHAT IS SELF-COMPASSION

To understand the word self-compassion, it would be helpful to comprehend what the word compassion means. Compassion means to feel sympathy or to suffer with.

It is a general view that the suffering of others, motivates us to feel compassion for them. Consider a situation, where you are on your way to your office, and you see a homeless person begging; you might stop to consider his adverse case. Your heart might feel like it has a connection with that of the beggar's. You do not feel like ignoring him, and you are urged by your inner self to help him in some way. That feeling is accurately described as compassion. It is clear from this example that compassion entails feelings of care, kindness, and understanding for the people in pain.

Self-compassion has the same attributes; the only difference is that compassion is turned inwards. Self-compassion is not just an individual feeling, and it has three essential dimensions; self-kindness, mindfulness, and common humanity.

Self-kindness

Self-compassion demands us to be understanding and warm to ourselves in sufferings and failure instead of criticizing oneself. One should recognize that experiencing the difficulties of life and being imperfect is inevitable, so we nurture and soothe ourselves when confronting pain instead of getting angry when we fall short of our aims. We should acknowledge our shortcoming and the fact that we cannot always achieve what we want. Otherwise, if we turn our mind away from this reality and deny it, the result is the suffering in the form of frustration, stress, and self-criticism. If this reality is acknowledged, we can generate emotions of care and kindness that can help us cope with the problem.

Mindfulness

Mindfulness is a receptive and nonjudgmental state of mind in which feelings and thoughts are observed as they may be, without denying them. The response to the negative thoughts about oneself is either agonizing over them or ignoring them.

When confronted by adversities we often try to solve the problem without recognizing the dire need to calm and comfort ourselves for the difficulties we are facing. The mental space that is provided by taking a mindful approach to our harsh feelings allows us to have greater emotional patience, perspective, and clarity.

Common Humanity

The biggest problem of self-judgment is that it makes us feel alone and isolated. When we come to know something about ourselves that we do not like, we see everyone else as perfect and view ourselves as inadequate. Focusing on our shortcomings renders us shortsighted, and we cannot see anything apart from our own so-called "worthless" self. We also may feel abnormal. When something is wrong, we are affected by it, and other people seem to handle it better. In such situations, self-compassion puts things in order and helps us to recognize the fact that other people also feel inadequate at different stages of their lives. We get to know that failures are an experience that everyone shares. This thought dramatically comforts us in adversities.

At this point, it is entirely necessary to know which acts are not to be mistaken with self-compassion. People often confuse self-compassion with self-pity, self-indulgence, and self-esteem.

Often people are reluctant to do self-compassion because they mistake it with self-pity. Self-pity is entirely different from self-compassion. If someone feels self-pity, they would inevitably become immersed in their adversities and problems and tend to forget that other people might also have the same issues. They would feel as if they were the one out of all the others who had problems. Self-pity is characterized by the ego-centric feelings of isolation and exaggerates the magnitude of personal distress. On the other hand in self-compassion people acknowledge that they are not the only one in harsh situations and this thought greatly comforts them.

An even greater stigma on self-compassion is that people think of it to be some self-indulgence. Some people believe that self-criticism is entirely necessary to motivate oneself. Otherwise, if they are too self-compassionate they will sit around wasting their time, is there any truth to this? It can be explained by the example of how parents motivate young ones. When parents care about their children and desire their well-being, do they indulge by allowing them to do whatever they want? No. They will make sure that their children eat well, brush their teeth, go to school regularly, finish their homework and sleep early because it is necessary for them to be healthy and live a good life. Their children will surely be motivated to reach their goals in life and can count on their parents' support even if they fail.

Now let's consider the situation where parents ruthlessly criticize their children when they mess up and tell them that they are failures, how is it going to make the children feel? Motivated, inspired, ready to achieve their goals? Certainly not. Constant criticism can make us feel depressed and worthless, not precisely the keep-moving-on mindset. Isn't it the same manner in which we treat ourselves? And somehow are led to believe that self-criticism is an effective motivator than self-compassion. That's the reason why self-criticism is often linked with self-handicapping and underachievement.

Distinguishing self-compassion from self-esteem is also essential. Self-esteem is the extent to which we tend to evaluate ourselves positively. It shows our liking for ourselves and is based on comparison with others. In popular cultures, having high self-esteem as compared to others means to think of oneself to be unique and above other average people. On the other hand, self-compassion is not characterized by positive evaluation or judgment. It focuses on interconnections instead of separateness. Moreover, it provides emotional stability.

Chapter 2

WHY YOU MIGHT LACK SELF-COMPASSION

Now that we see and know ourselves, or more importantly, have reached a higher degree of awareness towards ourselves, we are now capable of genuinely loving who we are. Having found out about our strengths and most especially our weaknesses, we are now capable of focusing on the things that we need to nurture in ourselves. We know now which parts of us we need to heal. Some of us might equate self-love with pride, but these two are things from very different worlds. Pride is tolerating one's negative aspects thinking it is self-love to preserve one's ego, but it is not. Self-love is when you decide to nurture and desire growth for yourself, no matter how uncomfortable that may be. It takes a lot of self-love for one to be able to do that. But believe me, if you haven't done so for yourself yet, self-love is perhaps the most beautiful thing you can ever give to yourself in this world. For it only means you give yourself absolute independence from the rest of the world. Being able to love yourself for who you are gives you the power not to need anyone's validation.

For one thing that everyone needs to learn, is that ultimately, our constant companion is our own self. No one else, not even our closest loved one, is going to stay with us all the time except ourselves. Hence, we must learn to enjoy our companionship. How many of us here love themselves so much they wouldn't dare hurt one's self? Not just physically, but mentally and spiritually. A lot of us here, are mean even to ourselves, maybe not intentionally but we do so all the same. How can that be? Well, whenever we tell ourselves negative things that in itself is already a form of self-abuse. Whenever we look in the mirror and conclude to ourselves for example that we are unattractive, isn't it that we feel bad in our self? And ironically, we felt bad in the first place by saying something negative about ourselves. If by any chance, you are that kind of person, isn't it that by doing so you become your own lousy companion? What's worse is that whenever someone else says negative things about you, you would believe them, not necessarily because it's true, but more so because you believe in it yourself.

Hence, self-love is practically self-positive reaffirmation. We must be able to love our selves so much that we are capable of self-compassion or self-empathy. To be able to treat ourselves with so much respect that we are incapable of doing anything remotely disrespectful to our beings. In other words, we are also our own best friends. Whenever we feel down or discouraged, we are the ones who lift and encourage ourselves to become more motivated. We are the ones who greatly strive to be able to get the things we want and desire most. Having lots of self-love then enables us to become mentally, emotionally, and spiritually independent. In other words, we strive to become what we want and need the most. Doing so, growing aware of the things that we want and need, physically, mentally, emotionally, and spiritually, we also then move towards the things that benefit us the most. Suddenly, we find ourselves giving less and less time doing things that don't help us grow as people. In turn, surrounding us with lots of self-love and attention, we feel a higher amount of satisfaction in our lives. As opposed to asking for all these things from other people. Most certainly they are going to fail us from time to time. Hence, it is of great convenience that we can rely on ourselves all the time.

Not that we are going to be discouraged from entrusting ourselves to other people. Paradoxically, becoming independent of other people's love is what allows us to love other people unconditionally, and more so, it is what makes us appreciate their passion, even more, knowing that we didn't also need it in the first place. Now, this level of self-love that I am talking about takes a lot of time to develop. Before we can achieve it, we need incredible amounts of self-awareness. Being able to figure ourselves out entirely that we know everything that we need in all aspects of our lives. And as we mentioned, this level of self-love makes us capable of unconditionally loving other people. For this self-love becomes the standard to which we love other people.

A good question would be, what is the best possible way that we may be able to create more self-love? How is that going to manifest? For us to know just that, what we need is self-compassion. When we are self-compassionate, then we can think about what's best for us. We become more aware of the things that we want and need the most, and so we consciously work towards giving ourselves precisely those things. Now, of course, this will depend on the personality of the person, the things that they want and need. But, what we have come to understand, is the fact that we want and need the most, is peace. For whatever situation we are in life that is the thing that we always look for. Some might say, it is happiness, but the thing is, we can't have joy if we do not have peace. For peace is the foundation for all the positive emotions or practically all the feelings that we have, without it is impossible for us to feel anything good.

About all of this, overall, we become more sensitive towards ourselves giving us the ability to have more empathy. And by practicing self-empathy, we are then also honed to become more thoughtful and compassionate towards others. As the ancient yet always entirely relevant saying goes, "Do unto others what you would want others to do unto you."

Chapter 3

MINDFUL SELF-COMPASSION

Mindfulness helps you build self-love. Before we delve into how mindfulness enables you to make self-love, let us understand mindfulness.

Mindfulness is the act of being present in every moment, concentrating on what you are doing at any point in time, and refusing to dwell on past mistakes and future worries.

How Mindfulness Helps You Build Self-Love

When you engage in mindful practices such as conscious breathing, meditation, yoga, etc., you focus your mind on the things you have been overlooking all your life. Mindfulness makes you more grateful for the ideas and abilities you have.

Mindfulness also enables you to take note of things that add value to your life; things you have always considered insignificant such as your ability to talk people into changing certain habits, your ability to make people smile amidst worries, your ability to come up with solutions to challenging puzzles, etc.

Mindfulness also helps you notice all the things you have going for you and enables you to love and respect whom you are.

How can you practice mindfulness to develop self-respect and improve self-love? Here are some ideas to guide you:

1: Know what you think, feel, and want most times

Mindful people keep track of their most dominant thoughts, feelings, and desires. When you become more aware of your thoughts and feelings, it becomes easier to control your flow of thoughts and emotions.

2: Separate your positive thoughts and opinions from the negative ones

Once you become mindful of your most dominant thoughts and feelings, you will be in a position to sieve your thoughts and separate the healthy from the unhealthy ones.

Imagine a deep hole beneath the surface of the earth where you can channel all thoughts that make building self-love challenging. Retain all positive thoughts and willingly replay them in your mind. You can make positive thoughts into some affirmations and repeat them as often as you can until they become a part of you.

3: Train yourself to become more mindful of what goes on around you

Making mindfulness a part of your daily life will increase self-love and the quality of life you live. Let us learn how you can make mindfulness a part of your daily life:

Practice Mindful Breathing

Mindful breathing is an aspect of mindfulness that helps you concentrate on how your breath cycles come and go. Conscious breathing begins with locating a suitable quiet spot free from any distractions. Anywhere around your home or office should be ideal provided the place is serene, secluded and conducive to helping you quickly master the art of concentration.

Once you find a location, settle into your most comfortable posture, and concentrate on your breathing taking in the whole whoosh sound as the air rushes in and out of your windpipe, the time it takes you to complete a cycle of breath, and how many breaths you can take in a minute. Do not think about anything else, only your breath matters at this point.

Develop a Mantra

A mantra is just a word or sound you repeat several times to help you focus and concentrate during your mindful exercises. Your mantra can be a word, a phrase, sentence, or just a sound.

Developing and focusing on a mantra during your mindful exercises can help you become grounded/centered enough to notice the most lovely and amazing things about yourself and life in general.

Your mantra can be one of the positive thoughts you created into an affirmation or any other thing you consider positive and motivating enough to make you love yourself more. It can be a thought centered on your signature strengths and talents.

This mantra should form the basis of your focus as soon as you become accustomed to your breath and its pattern. Your mantra can be something like, "Im going to win, "Nothing can stop me, or something like "I'm the best singer, athlete, student, employee, actor, or investor."

Be mindful of everything else

The state of mindfulness should not stop at your breathing and mantra; you should be able to transfer it to every other activity you engage in during the day. These activities should include the ones you participate in at home and the ones you fight in when you are at the office or school.

When you take note of what goes on around you during the day, and how you handle issues that crop up in your line of work, the respect you have for yourself will grow, and naturally, your self-esteem will start on a bullish run.

Practice Self-Respect

Practicing self-respect is one of the most important aspects of practicing self-love. If you cannot respect yourself, it will be impossible to love yourself for who you are. You must find something to appreciate about yourself before you can find something to enjoy about yourself. How can you practice self-respect? Here are some tips:

1: Carry yourself with dignity

The way you carry yourself tells a lot about how much self-respect you have, and influences the respect people give to you. Take a queue from charismatic people and the way they give respect to themselves.

You can start by always walking briskly with your head held high and your shoulders squared. Even while seated, sit like someone who is sure of himself/herself by sitting straight with your legs stretched in front of you, hands clasped, and on your lap.

2: Present yourself in the most respectable way

There is a direct correlation between how you present yourself and how people address you. A great deal of how you give respect to yourself has to do with what you wear and how you wear it. One school of thought says others address you depending on how you dress. This is something to consider maybe.

3: Have a high opinion of yourself

You do not need all the money, fame, or success in the world before you start seeing the royalty in you. Always treat yourself as if you have already attained the heights you are aiming for in life. Imagine the future you are working towards and see yourself there. This will increase your self-respect and self-love.

Chapter 4

KNOWING YOURSELF

Before you can practice self-love, you need to practice self-acceptance. To do so, you need to understand what self-acceptance is.

Self-acceptance involves accepting yourself for whom you genuinely are irrespective of your faults, weakness, and all. Self-acceptance means acknowledging your flaws and coming to terms with the fact that you have those flaws but understanding that these flaws do not have enough gravity to make you a failure in life. Self-acceptance is all about embracing your qualities and flaws and feeling satisfied and confident even when the odds are against you.

Self-acceptance precedes self-love. Practicing self-acceptance enables you to practice unreserved self-love. Once you accept yourself for whom you are, loving your flawed, imperfect self.

How can you practice self-acceptance to improve your self-love? Here are some steps you can take:

1: Weigh your strengths against your weaknesses

Get a piece of paper and a pen and use them to create something you can always refer to as a way to assess your progress. On one side of the article, write everything you consider as your strengths, and on the other side of the paper, write everything you think are your weaknesses.

2: Accept your shortcomings and commit to overcoming them

Once you make a list of your strengths and weaknesses, come to terms with the fact that you have some severe flaws to deal with and specific strengths you can leverage to make your life better.

It is not enough to accept you have specific weaknesses, you must also decide to work on them. If you do not try to get rid of your weaknesses, your many imperfections may make it hard for you to love yourself. For each gap, set a goal to overcome it within a specified period, and never stop trying until you master that weakness.

3: Acknowledge your strengths and build upon them

It is easy to love yourself when you have several strong things going for you and life is good. Discovering your powers and acknowledging them gives you several compelling reasons why self-love is something you have to pursue.

Your strengths are the things you discover you can do without waiting for anyone to teach or prompt you to do them. For instance, if you have the charisma to address large audiences and leave a lasting impression, then confidence is one of your greatest strengths.

4: Convince yourself you have all you need to live a great life

Philosophers have described the mind of man as a tabular slide. This means that your account is an empty slate and whatever you write on it stays. If you start telling yourself you have all you need to be happy, fulfilled, and successful, your mind will readily believe that, and start working with that perspective as it seeks ways to make your dreams come true.

If you practice the above four steps, you should start wholly accepting the person you are, irrespective of your flaws and because you know your strengths, you will feel intricately motivated to pursue self-love, your goals, dreams, and aspirations.

Once this happens, you will be one step closer to being a perennial self-lover.

Chapter 5

DEVELOPING SELF-COMPASSION

The importance of self-compassion in our lives cannot be denied. Those who refuse this reality and try to find effectiveness in excessive self-esteem and self-criticism or follow any other negative path in efforts of overcoming their problems, they are lead to the valley of desperation and anxiety by life. Nowadays due to high competition in every sphere of life, many people often get their focus diverted from their inner-self, and their sole focus is on their worldly matters. As a result, if they fail at any stage of their lives, they are engulfed by epidemics of anxiety, loneliness, addiction, and depression.

Social Anxiety Disorder:

It is usually observed that people who do not feel compassionate towards themselves are often involved in self-criticism. Many problems in the social and personal life of a person can arise due to self-criticism and lack of self-compassion. The most common and alarming disorder that is caused due to these are known as Social Anxiety Disorder (SAD) or Social Phobia. It falls in the category of mental disorders. In this type of disease, the subject unreasonably fears the social situations and their results. They are afraid of the criticism others might give them, in short, they become negatively over-conscious about themselves. All this anxiety can lead them to an attack of panic. They tend to run away from the realities of life and endure extreme distress. Studies also suggest that people who are suffering from SAD can't think clearly, they have false beliefs and keep negative opinions about others. Their public speaking skills are also rusted.

Academic Procrastination

It might be difficult to believe, but people who are not self-compassionate are often procrastinators. A majority of such people are the students, who are at their crucial stages of life where self-compassion is needed the most. Procrastinators usually delay their essential pieces of work and are indulged in pleasure-seeking activities. Academic procrastination can lead to delay in home work, inability to complete crucial projects and assignments in time. It is not necessary for anyone to be in adversities to practice self-compassion. Even in normal situations like daily academic routines self-compassion is also useful; you can try to motivate your inner self to work to achieve the best possible outcome.

Increase in Depression

Depression is the most common type of disorder in people that isolate themselves. Gender-wise depression is most common in women as compared to men. In despair a person thinks negatively about themselves and the people around them; their perception about others is often negative, and they tend to lose faith and trust in others. Many of these actions over a period can lead a person to depression; the most common of them is self-criticism. Beating ourselves up every time with self-criticism when we commit mistakes is the biggest mistake in itself. Instead of doing you any good, it is likely to deteriorate motivation, and the instinct of facing problems. For those people who think that self-criticism is going to motivate you, to be honest self-criticism is quite painful, and subconsciously, its outcome is the most dangerous.

Lack of Gratitude:

Lack of gratitude can be observed in people that are not compassionate towards themselves. In sufferings and adversities most of our life is spent silently complaining to ourselves and others, this means that we are not grateful for what we have in hand. This leads us to forget about the great thing that is currently present in our lives. Lack of gratitude in your personal life can increase your depression while in social life it can hurt your relationships with others.

Feeling Rushed

Lack of self-compassion can increase the feeling of urgency considerably. Throughout the day we experience a sense of rushing on to the next thing or task. We want to move quickly, so whilst working we tend to switch to subsequent communication, next task, next tab, etc. All of this becomes a constant source of stress and tension.

Distraction

Lack of self-compassion quite often results in distraction in everyday matters. Nowadays or live are super-distracted, and we often waste our essential time. This distraction depicts the suffering in our lives; we do not want to complete our tasks because of the thoughts of failure. Distraction momentarily gives us comfort.

Rejection Sensitivity

Rejection sensitivity might be the most common problem in compassion-less people. We are afraid of the outcomes of the events and perceive different results and adapt ourselves to cope with the matters on the bases of our wrong expectations. Rejection sensitive people damage their interpersonal skills and are most likely to get involved in verbal hostility. Adolescent girls are most likely to have these problems as compared to the male gender.

Most of us here have made so many mistakes, some of which are very dreadful, that we sometimes are unable to forgive even ourselves. A lot of times, it comes from other people, wherein they would be telling us that we've done something very wrong, that they tell us we are unworthy of forgiveness. Us, lacking self-love, we choose to believe them. Doing so, we are permitting ourselves to be miserable. We are offering the world an excuse that it is alright for us to suffer, more so, that it is natural for us to be experiencing negative things. A license to bear so to speak.

But of course, before we can forgive ourselves, we must first have to admit that we have made a mistake, that we have done something wrong. Acceptance of our imperfection. To tell ourselves it is okay that indeed we are capable of committing an error, just like everyone else. Forgive ourselves for the fact that we are only human. We do not know everything at any given point in time. We are always open to making mistakes. People may condemn us or punish us for allowing ourselves to do so but that is usually very hypocritical of them. No one is perfect, that needs no reassurance. Every single person on Earth has made a mistake. Not even the greatest of personalities here on Earth are free of them, to which perhaps what has made them the greatest is the fact that they probably have made a million mistakes. Because the thing is, making a mistake shouldn't be a negative thing in the first place. It is right in the sense that it is through these mistakes that we can learn. These mistakes become the inspiration from where the next much better versions of ourselves will come from.

The most important thing is that we are humble enough to learn from these mistakes. This, in itself, is a form of self-love. It won't matter if the whole world has already forgiven us for some mistake we have done, if we haven't forgiven ourselves yet for whatever it is that we have done wrong. To make it easier for us to imagine the benefits of forgiving ourselves, and simultaneously those around us, merely visualize that whenever we forgive, we also let go of an equivalent anchor that has been tied to our souls. Hence, the more that we do the act of forgiving, the more that our soul becomes lighter. Consider as well that forgiving is also the same as opening doors and windows that become pathways for blessings to come into our lives.

Forgiveness, as well, is the ultimate act of grace. Being able to pardon the mistakes of others and one's own mistakes is something that is close to divinity. As the famous saying says that to err is human yet to forgive is divine. Only someone who has a truly generously loving heart and a mind full of understanding is capable of doing something close to a miracle. In contrast to when we choose to punish or condemn ourselves or those who have made mistakes. Just imagine, how someone would feel if they were scheduled for the death penalty on this very minute but then just seconds before execution, someone calls and announces that this person has been pardoned. By this analogy, forgiving yourself is like giving you a second chance at life. Whenever we are condemning ourselves, it feels as if we aren't alive because our self-worth is so low.

Forgiveness then is most definitely an act of self-compassion. Being compassionate enough towards one's self that we choose to acknowledge the fact that we are merely humans capable of mistakes. Not only forgiveness for ourselves but others, knowing especially that to forgive is not just an act we do for others but mostly for our own piece of mind. When we choose not to forgive, we want instead to carry on hate, which then only leads to anger. Such emotions that at this point we are already very aware is not good for us mentally. Holding on to these things is like holding on to a bomb waiting to explode. So to be compassionate to ourselves.

Pride is something that doesn't let us forgive. Pride, which gives us this notion of having so much self-importance, allows us to think that we are incapable of making mistakes, hence making us incapable of seeing that we even need to forgive ourselves. More so, pride makes us feel that we are better than other people, it makes us arrogant to the point of thinking so highly of ourselves that we think other people do not deserve our forgiveness. This completely goes against our self-compassion hence we must be thoroughly aware of our pride. Then, of course, make the conscious decision to rid ourselves of it. To forgive is to let go of ego, become more selfless, and put more emphasis and importance towards peace more than pride. More and more people are choosing to forgive instead of hate. More and more people want to hold flowers instead of guns. Can you imagine a world that is more like this? There will be less hate, anger, and violence, and consequently means more peace, love, and unity. A more self-compassionate and self-loving world capable of making miracles, just because we choose to forgive. Just because we let go of what is unnecessary and focus instead on what we should truly value.

How many more relationships must fail because of our inability to forgive? Let us say no more. In the end, choosing not to forgive as we have mentioned only hurts us the most. So go on, let us do ourselves a favor and forgive. We most definitely deserve peace more than retribution.

Chapter 6

Dealing with Emotions

Have you ever put anyone's needs before yours and found yourself resenting them for it after? This is a sign you were trying to be helpful instead of genuinely kind. If you do not cover your own needs first, your resentment will inevitably grow towards the other person you have helped out. You may find you start passive-aggressive actions or snide remarks on your behalf. Jealousy is what kills, and often the other person can sense a type of aggressiveness from you towards them and are often oblivious to what they've done.

My friend John is a prestigious lawyer in America; he was talking to me about a pattern he found in a lot of domestic abuse cases. He said on his first case in this field how he walked in to talk to the suspect. Expecting to see a violent man before him. He had seen the case reports and the horrific photographs of the woman who had been beaten. However when he walked in and started to interview the man in question he was shocked. The man was so friendly, helpful and just seemed to be incapable of such a crime. So much so, John had to walk out and double-check if this was the right man he had seen sitting before him. John said over his long career, how he had seen a lot of cases exactly like this, and he couldn't understand the pattern. He then figured it out a theory for it one day. These men were so incapable of expressing their feelings or standing up for themselves that they suppressed it all. Them being nice caused them to receive years and years of abuse which they failed to deal with properly. The rage built up and built up until one day they snapped, and all that rage had to be released. This was not a healthy or kind way to deal with this problem and very severely affected the lives for all involved. When in a verbally abusive relationship like this man was, blame has to be put on both parties. If we don't speak up and stand up for ourselves, we encourage more of the same behavior from the abuser. In a lot of these cases, the men involved were victims who invited their abuse to a degree, when they didn't express how they felt. Which led from them being a victim to becoming the abuser. It would never have happened if they had shown how they felt. If their wives continued this behavior, it was also their responsibility to leave. You see if we state we are not ok with something and the other person knows this and continues anyway, it is our responsibility to have the self-compassion to leave this person behind, as we don't need people like this in our lives. By doing this, showing yourself compassion, your self-esteem will be free to grow; if you don't, it will remain trapped amongst the thorns of your resentment.

Often being kind, is the hard thing to do but it is almost always the best thing to do.

How To Deal With Resentment Destroyin Relationships

As we talked about before, resentment is destroying relationships. If we fail to make clear boundaries how we expect other people to behave it is not their fault if they continue to act in a way you dislike. To help prevent resentment even being created in the first place, we must make sure our needs are covered before helping others. Once we do this, we help people from a place where we are centered and emotionally grounded.

The Contracts We Make In Our Heads

When putting others first we often unconsciously create a contract with that person in our heads. This contract should be disregarded however as only one party knows about it, that party is you. Nice people often tend to do good things for others. However, this can usually be followed by resentment towards the person they helped. If you have ever felt this way, it was because you created a contract in your head.

An example would be, say you have a friend who could do with losing weight. So you draw up a diet plan for them to follow and spend a good bit of time on it. A few weeks later, you find out they have not been developing the diet plan; you feel a strong feeling of resentment towards them. If you think this way, you were not coming from a genuinely kind place, as there is never resentment stemming from kindness. It is a lot more likely, coming from a place of being nice. A mindset of, "If I fix you, you have to like me." The contract in this situation was, "I'll draw up this diet plan, but you have to follow it." The only thing is the other person didn't know about this arrangement, and it was never openly stated. This would have been different if before you had spent the time writing the plan out, you added conditions. If you were to say, "If I take the time to write this out for you, will you take it seriously and follow it?" This way the person will either agree or disagree. If they do accept and break the arrangement, at least they will have known they have, and you would not do something like this again for them. This way there are no hidden terms, and if the person doesn't follow the arrangement, it is openly known by both parties. The point here is not that you have to make everything into this deal format. It is that we should value our own time and if we are going to give it up for someone, it should be something that's important to them, and they take seriously. Otherwise, you are merely saying to yourself your time is less important than theirs. We also should allow people to help themselves or wait until they ask you for help. As this is coming from a much more emotionally centered place. Nice people often tend to help someone who maybe hasn't asked for it or maybe doesn't even want it.

When we start to value our time, our self-esteem will consequently go up. When we recognize our own needs as necessary, it will raise our self-esteem. When we come from a place where we value our time, express what we would expect the other person to do as a result of our help, if there is anything, we can then help them out of a place of kindness and resentment-free.

Remember to monitor your feelings. If you feel resentment, ask yourself why, and then take the appropriate action. It's often hard to look at our good deeds so critically. However, it is the best thing you can do for your relationships. If your friends or family care about you, they would rather you be honest with them than secretly going through periods of resenting them without their knowledge. Put yourself in their shoes, I don't know about you, but I would rather my friends told me if they are not ok with doing something if it meant avoiding them from resenting me. Then once we address the issue, our relationships get a lot stronger and more stable.

How We Talk To Ourselves

Words are powerful and can drastically change the way we perceive events. We are often our own harshest critics at a time where we need self-compassion. After our failures, we usually go through long periods of reliving the events in our head unable to let go of them. What makes this worse is what we chose to focus on and the words we use when we speak to ourselves. There is a place for the use of this pain to motivate us to do better. However, there are times when we need to show compassion to ourselves and sometimes do what is hardest of all and forgive ourselves.

Often we speak to ourselves worse than we would talk to our worst enemy. However, nothing beneficial comes of this. Instead, we need to take responsibility for what we say to ourselves. When we take control of this, talk to yourself as you would to a close friend going through the same ordeal. Often people will say they need this abuse as motivation. However, it had exactly the opposite than the desired effect. When we are too harsh of critics, it leads to depression mind states which make it difficult to do or achieve anything difficult.

Whereas if we are encouraging to ourselves, we can use this as fuel for motivation and change in our life if we see fit.

When an event we did not desire has happened, it can be hard to let go of. Even years down the line, we still carry this pain with us, unable to let it go and forget it. We can only ever learn from our mistakes. However, it makes no sense to carry the pain on with us as we move forward with our lives. To do this, first, we need to acknowledge and accept these events happened. One of the easiest ways to do this is to write it down on a piece of paper. Then once you have taken, they have arrived and have written it down, tear up the piece of paper. This sounds stupid and illogical. However, the thing with our emotions and dealing with them is that they are often irrational. It's incredible how useful this little trick is, and I urge you to try it.

We also tend to feel isolated when we're not feeling too good. We feel as if we are the only one that feels this way. However, that is never the case. There is a famous saying, "The more personal a problem, the more universal it is." When we're feeling low, we can force ourselves to remember other people think like this as well and if others can get through it, so can we. It's ok to feel this way; it's just a sign we may need to change something in our lives. It is important to know we are never alone.

Self-Acceptance Exercise

In this exercise, we will work with accepting ourselves in this present moment for who we are, faults and all. It should be practiced throughout a couple of weeks. There is a kind of paradox in this area of self-help, as in one aspect you are accepting yourself for who you are and in the other, you are trying to improve yourself. However, the way I deal with this is, as long as I am working on being my best self, then I can accept myself as I am. This way you grow and learn to take yourself for the way you are.

It's remarkable how much a small change on your inside can have such a profound influence on your life and external reality as a whole. Our mind influences our outside world, and this is where we need to change to get long lasting significant results. The outer is often a superficial side, a bi-product of what is going on inside.

Ok to start, put your attention in this present moment. Pay attention to the sensations in your body and notice how they feel. Pay attention to your breathing. Feel the air going past your lips, see if the wind is warmer or colder as it comes out from your lungs past your lips. Now I want you to bring up a time where you felt love for a person or an event. Feel that sensation throughout your body. Extend it throughout your body. Now take this love and apply it to the other parts of your personality. Think of the role of you that's funny, use it to that side, don't logically think of what you are doing, just doing it. Give this part of your personality your complete undivided unconditional love. Now take the part of your character that feels shame, conjure up that feeling and then give your full unconditional love towards this part of your style. Now bring up the part of your personality that has overreacted with anger towards something, and give your unconditional love to this part of your character.

Now continue to do this for all the different parts of your psychology. I'll list some here:

- ❖ The role of you that has felt embarrassed.
- ❖ The part of you that has a high work ethic.

- ❖ The lazy part of you.
- ❖ The sad part of your psychology.
- ❖ The happy part of your psychology.
- ❖ The part of you that has felt rejected.
- ❖ The part of you that is sexually frustrated.
- ❖ The part of you that is confident.
- ❖ The part of you that has felt guilty.

and any others you can think of.

Continue to do this whenever you have any free time regularly, and you'll be amazed how your psychology will change in a few weeks. You are wholeheartedly accepting yourself, flaws and all.

Self-Forgiveness

More often than not the hardest person for us to forgive is often ourselves. We can have so much trouble letting go sometimes even when it's of no help to anyone. All we can do is learn from our mistakes. Here I will show you how to learn to forgive yourself.

So to deal with guilt, we must understand why we feel it. We feel guilt due to two reasons: We believe that our actions have caused a bad result and that we were responsible for that result. So to deal with sin, we need to change at least one of these.

Us as humans haven't developed the Godlike ability to predict precisely what will happen due to our actions. We are limited in that way. So thus we cannot be held responsible for that result as it is out of our control. This is especially true if you set out with good intentions.

We also don't know the ramifications of our actions further down the line. By us causing an adverse event to happen in someone's life, we could be leading them onto a path of something better down the road. Your actions could lead them to find the love of their life or be happier than ever. We never really know the full scale of events that happen to us in our lives. So thus we can't competently claim that our actions have led to a bad result.

I am not saying to take responsibility, what I am saying is guilt often serves no purpose after an initial phase. We must merely, set out with good intentions, learn from our actions and try to implement our new found knowledge in future decisions.

Building Unshakable Self-Esteem

Many of us derive our self-esteem from achieving specific results or feeling better than someone. It is the norm in our society that being average is terrible. If you called someone average, they would be more than likely offended. So for a lot of us, we derive our self-esteem from us being better than other people. However, this is a foolish way to view life. We were born with self-esteem, it is our natural state, yet, more often or not, specific influences on our life have drilled it out of us.

So how do we start to regain our self-esteem? I've talked about in the previous chapters, however here I want to add something which I believe to be crucial to not only self-worth but long-term sustainable self-esteem. It is living a life of principles, rather than a life of results. Having a high work ethic for your job is a principle. Getting promotions is a result. Having good intentions is a principle, people liking you due to something you did for them is a result. More often than not, living by principles will gear you towards your achievement. However we must remember a lot of life is out of our control, the only thing we can control is our actions.

An example of a person, living life by results would be: Say you set out to help someone. However, something out of your control went wrong, and it ended up causing them more hassle instead of helping them. Often people would take this very badly, and it would negatively affect their self-esteem. However, someone with principle-based self-esteem wouldn't consider this wrong. As you had good intentions, you were not knowledgeable or in control of what happened so don't feel bad about it. If it is necessary, surely apologize to the person. However, don't view yourself as a bad person because something terrible has happened. After it has happened, definitely learn from your mistakes and use that knowledge to decide how you would do it differently the next time but don't get hung up on it. This would be entirely different if you set out with bad intentions, however. This is where integrity comes into play. We always know what the right thing to do is. We should always follow this feeling no matter what, as otherwise, we compromise our integrity and thus our self-esteem. It can be comfortable standing up for what you believe to be right a lot of the time but sometimes it is tough, and so these are the times that matter the most.

To live a life of principles, we must first know what our policies are. It is worth spending time writing these down and writing down what we believe in. Even knowing these principles will make a massive difference to our lives. So often we can be put in a situation where we have to think so fast that we make a decision we later regret. It is a lot easier when you know who you are and what you stand for, however. Once you know the principles in your life that you follow, then follow them no matter what. Integrity is a vital part of how we view ourselves. So start taking the importance of the results you get and focus on living a life of integrity by following your core principles.

Chapter 7

THE POWER OF SELF-COMPASSION

Nowadays we might not have enough time to sit down and talk to ourselves. Our lives have become so complicated that we do not know what we are chasing, why we are wasting our time and what we actually want. All we are taught is to be successful and lead a content life, but we are never told what successful life means and what sort of life is best. We work day and night to find that success, and eventually, we start to realize that we have been on the wrong path and we have been after the mistaken ambitions of life. The result is that we end up in adversities and it's too late to go back and change the past. We are beaten by ourselves to our knees and getting up seems to be impossible in such adversities.

At such adverse stages of life, it is quite natural that we think of ourselves to be failures and we are often jealous of other people out there that are having a good time while you suffer. So at this stage thinking that we are the problem and showing self-pity towards oneself is a foolish thing. This leads to many misleading thoughts, self-criticism and sometimes people giving up their efforts. They are indulged in self-sabotage and distress. The anxieties are ever increasing, and the amount of stress on us is quite alarming. We think that this is the end of life, but really it is far from it.

In Asian cultures, man is considered to be a sculpture made out of mistakes. Everyone makes mistakes, and somehow it is our nature to feel regret over them. The point here to ponder is that no one knows what the future holds for them and no sensible person would commit mistakes willingly. Everything that happens is our fate. If we could know about the future, no one would commit errors. Everyone would have been perfect and flawless.

This is not the case, and mistakes and the subsequent sufferings are a part of everyone's life. Our imperfections lead us to the adversities and sufferings. But our fault is not to be blamed because we have to live with the notion that everyone can commit mistakes and no one can lead a happy life forever. Our primary focus after admitting these facts should be not to give up and keep on making our efforts to fend off the problems and sufferings and try to achieve some harmony in our lives. To deal with your adverse problems in some positive way is the beauty of self-compassion.

At these stages of life the most suitable companion that can help you in regaining confidence, willpower, and a restore a sense of purpose in life, is self-compassion. Admitting our shortcomings and still trying to keep ourselves on the move are nothing less than courage and bravery. Moreover, the sufferings and challenges give meaning to life.

The human progress towards stability is not something that happens overnight; instead, it is a progressive, stable and genuine advance towards the peaks of life. We cannot expect to get out of the downs of life overnight. Instead, it takes willpower, vision, endurance, patience and last but not the least self-compassion. The main conclusion is that admitting one's mistakes, considering sufferings to be a part of life and making the utmost effort to get up on your feet and face the adversities is quite a difficult task in itself, but those who are up to this task are the ones who emerge out victorious.

How many times have we concerned ourselves with the past or the future? Lost sleep over these things that do not exist in the first place? It may be hard to believe for some, but think about it, the past and the future are merely figments of our imagination. Many of us have experienced anxiety over the thought of something horrible that happened in the past, or something equally as terrible in the future can relate very well to what I'm saying. Sometimes, we think these two things are so real we let it affect us to a certain degree. The most common perhaps is not being able to sleep thinking about a past scenario wherein something unpleasant happened to us, or imagining a future event wherein we feel about something genuinely disastrous that could happen. Since usually this happens when we are about to sleep and relax, but our mind says something else and keeps playing these scenes in our head as if it were happening right that moment. Right now, if we were to think about a past or future event, notice very well that it is only happening inside of our minds. The history and future, in essence, are merely illusions, projections of the brain.

Whenever we think about a past or a future situation, we have to realize within ourselves that it is but an illusion deeply. It's just that sometimes whenever we are thinking about a past or a future situation, depending on what we are imagining, it can be quite overwhelming for us hence we are pulled into that chain of thought. But if we try to relax and see these situations as they are, illusions, it loses its power over us, and we become capable of taking a step back and stop ourselves from imagining these situations. Thinking about the past and the future is merely a program we have embedded within our minds as a means to warn us of negative things that have happened in the past and may occur in the future for us to be able to prevent them in the present. In other words, they are merely warning signs, no more no less. Except, what happens to us is that we accept these supposed to be warning signs more than we should, we believe them to be real at that exact moment we are thinking about them, that's why they end up affecting us when they shouldn't be.

Our projections of the future themselves are a form of memory, for most of the time we base them on past events. For example, we think that we are going to fail in the future basing it on a recent event wherein we have also failed. We must be vigilant that what happens in the present depends mostly on what we do during the present time, not memories of the past and the future. We have to be aware that everything is merely an outcome of how we deal with the present moment.

Our primary focus for this chapter is for us to become grounded in the present moment, that which we also call "now." Consider, that if we are undisturbed by thoughts of the past and the future, what is always left is this present moment. And within this present moment, coupled with awareness, we find we aren't as miserable as our thoughts of past and future lead us to be. Relating it to the idea of suffering, we suffer because focusing on the history and tomorrow is to focus on the things we do not already have, considering these things are just basically figments of our imagination. In contrast to focusing on the present moment, wherein we can concentrate on the things we already have. More specifically, the power that we have within us to direct what we can and not do during this specific moment. Right now, we can most definitely choose what we wish to do. Although perhaps there can be limitations depending on each of our situations and status in life, the most important thing is the fact that we can choose. That choice in itself is the ultimate power that the present moment gives us. And the more that we exercise that power to decide, the more that we can practice it.

Now, if we think about it, we will finally realize that the only time we ever really have is always this "now" moment. There was never really a time that we have lived anywhere else in time but now. And from this point on we should be completely aware of the fact that the past and future are merely concepts that we have of time. Forms of memories that we only think up in our minds that distract us from the present moment, and the more that we separate ourselves from the present moment, the more that we open ourselves into suffering, into states of being away from self-love and self-compassion. Perhaps, you might ask, what if you are thinking about a past or a future memory in which there is the presence of self-love or self-compassion? Both still focuses on the idea that during the current moment there is no self-love or self-compassion and instead we look for them within these memories.

So, instead of fantasizing over illusory moments of past and future, we must be constantly aware of the present moment. For us to be able to consistently create and open ourselves to the infinite possibilities and opportunities that are available to us always within the present moment. The only time we can ever generate and manifest real and concrete actions that enable or moves us towards the things that we want. We cannot have true peace and genuine moments of self-compassion or self-love just imagining it in our minds, we have to create it constructively within the reality of the present moment, and there is no other way around it. It will not go away, in fact, we are only running away from these problems if we are going to live in thoughts of past and future. So, I sincerely urge you, be here, now. Claim the power that is within the present moment and from this create for yourself the reality that you truly want. Such displeasing thoughts of scenarios of past and future are merely guides that point us towards the present moment that we truly want. They are far from real, only if we act upon them can they become real.

So far, a lot of what we discussed, all boils down to these two motivating forces, which are fear and love.

Every time we listen to negative thought and let it consume us, fear is what we are looking to. Every time we worry over something, isn't it fear written all over it? Fear that something terrible is going to happen. Doubt that we are going to lose something. Doubt that we are undeserving of something. Doubt that we are not going to make it, that we are going to fail. Fear that we are not going to be accepted and Fear of what other people think.

Every negative thing in this world stems down to fear. While every positive thing branches out from love. Realize, that if we are being directed by fear more than love, we also address ourselves to live miserable and pathetic lives. Instead of us going after the things we want in life, we go ahead and become the number one antagonist in our lives by believing that we can't make it ourselves. We feel we fear that we do not have the necessary gifts to do what we want. We fear that we are going to fail. We fear that the things that we wish to do are impossible to achieve and cannot be done. So, if we let go of these fears, and dare to choose love instead, love in the sense that we believe in ourselves enough to have faith that we are capable of achieving the things that we want, we become our greatest ally. This way, in contrast to listening to our fears, we end up giving up on ourselves even though we haven't even tried to give ourselves a chance at succeeding. Yes, indeed it is a possibility that we may fail, there are a lot of reasons why it's going to be hard, but we are just going to ignore these things more so because failure is not the end of the world but only just a speed bump in life.

Our relationship with other people is also significantly affected by the play between fear and love. If we are being led by fear, our trust and affection towards other people also substantially decreases. We are afraid to trust or love other people because we fear that they are going to disappoint us. We fear that they are not going to like us back or return our trust. Whether it is a personal or a business relationship, we are not given room to thrive because we let fear command us and our actions. Hence, for us to have a beautiful, thriving relationship not just with ourselves but the people around us, we must learn to let go of fear. Or more appropriately, we must learn to have the proper courage to face these fears. To have so much courage that we are capable of saying, so what if I fail? So what if they disappoint me? So what if things may go wrong? So are all the things I'm striving for worth it anyway? That's right, loving ourselves enough is also synonymous to tough love, we must be willing to go through hardships and failures just so we can give ourselves the things that we love, things that we very much deserve. Realize that love is indeed on the other side of fear. If we cross that beyond our concerns, we find love and every beautiful thing that also comes with it, peace, happiness, abundance, and much more.

Furthermore, connecting it with everything that we have conferred up to now, fear and love is a present factor in all of them. First and foremost, with regards to suffering, we have discussed that what makes us suffer is the idea of losing something. Hence that is the fear that we feel whenever we are threatened to miss something. It may not be the direct solution to the imminent threat that we are about to lose something, but it is the most effective way we are going to be able to push through and more efficiently successfully acquire more of whatever that is that we are losing at the current moment. Better that we are working on what we want calm and composed than to go about panicking and worrying which considerably lessens our chances at being successful.

Next, one of the main reasons or perhaps the only reason we choose not to forgive, as we have previously discussed, is pride. Now, satisfaction as a reason why we want not to overlook is practically also an offspring of fear. Whenever we choose not to bestow forgiveness upon ourselves or another that is because we fear that we are not getting the respect and love that we deserve, hence we respond with such displeasure, and so we say, "No, I cannot forgive you." But if we already give to ourselves the love and respect that we do deserve, we do not need to deprive anyone of forgiveness anymore for we are already fulfilled from within. It is also pretty much the same situation whenever we choose not to give ourselves self-love.

Lastly, when it comes to choosing our self-identity, what stops us from adopting the highest form of self-reflection, the idea of "I am," is, of course, fear. As well as the idea of transcending from the body and towards the soul. We cannot adopt these ideas because we fear it is not possible. We think "I am only this body, it is impossible for me to become the soul" and so we choose to stay at the body.

So, no matter how crippling and influential our fears may be, always dare to choose love. Do not listen to these haunting screams of terror and instead open your ears to the beautiful melody that love plays for us. To listen to fear is to give up on the possibility of the good things in life, doing so we automatically revoke our right towards achieving, but if we listen to love and at least try, we increase our chances at a huge percent. Even if at the times that we fail, the fact that at least we have been attempting, gives us a sense of fulfillment no amount of fear can ever provide us. Love yourself enough to decide that we are worthy and deserving of the life that we want regardless of the doubt that we may not achieve it

Here in this chapter, we are going to magnify on the interdependence of our thoughts, emotions, and actions. To accentuate on just how powerful these things are as influences in our lives. This idea has already been presented in our other chapters, but here we are going to expand on it much more comprehensively. Let us start with our thoughts, which are the starting point of everything that happens in our lives. For all of us who are believers of God, we can say that the creation of the world in itself was ignited because God thought of creating us. In essence, then, the world, the universe, is God's idea manifested into reality. Now, if that is not enough evidence especially if you're not a believer of God, let us instead consider everything else in the world which is made by man. The radio, a television, your high-end laptop, the vehicle that you drive, up to the simple handkerchief that we use to wipe our faces with, these things are all inventions of man that started as an idea. Someone thought about them and decided to follow that thought and try to create an exact copy of that idea into reality. Many of course have somehow failed to get their ideas to manifest but look at the world now filled with so many successful designs that have turned into real concrete things that we can see, hold, and experience. This is precisely why in the starting chapters we have so vigorously highlighted on being able to control our thoughts. Starting with self-awareness which allows us to become conscious of our dreams. Talking about the idea of suffering and past and future as ideas that create illusions in our minds and hinders us from being able to take control of our thoughts. Up to the concept of meditation which completes the process, allowing us the opportunity of fully regaining control over our minds and consequently our thoughts.

To which now, having controlled our thoughts, or at least having been enlightened on just how important it is for us to have control over our thoughts, let us start to discuss more extensively about our emotions. For in a way we have already discussed this in our earlier chapters and to be more specific, the effects of our thoughts towards our emotions. If you have not realized by now, self-compassion, self-love, forgiveness, and most especially, suffering, are forms of emotions. These things are basic emotions that we feel that stems or originates from our thoughts. Self-compassion, to start with, is an emotion that we feel whenever we think about having sympathy and concern for ourselves. It is what we feel whenever we are moved by the idea of ourselves experience some suffering or misfortune. If in the first place, we did not have any idea of what suffering or misfortune is, we wouldn't feel self-compassion towards ourselves in the first place, nor compassion for other people. If we did not have an idea of what it is like to feel pain, isn't it that we would feel indifferent towards it? If we did not have the idea or the knowledge that people who have not eaten for days would feel starving, we would not feel one single bit of empathy towards them at all. Let alone if we did not know what being hungry is about in the first place. To give another example, let us also talk about forgiveness. The idea of forgiveness, to begin with, is very much connected to the idea or thought that someone has wronged or harmed us. If in actuality, we did not have the concept that we are capable of being wronged or harmed by others, then we are not going to feel hate towards anyone in the first place. There is no one to forgive right from the start, yet, since we have such an idea, we then are capable of feeling hate or displeasure towards others hence we are also capable of feeling, or it is necessary for us also to feel forgiveness towards others.

To make things even clearer, let us now also mention suffering. Isn't it, as we have discussed, that suffering is something that we feel whenever we think that we are losing something or in a way when we think that harm is being done to us? If, in the beginning, we did not have the idea of what suffering is like in the first place, then do you think we are still going to feel such suffering? Now, for us to have a clearer understanding of the connection between our thoughts and emotions, let us now also discuss the feeling of happiness. Isn't it so that we become happy whenever we think of the things that we think are beneficial for us? Like for example having delicious food to eat, a nice warm home to stay in, or simply having enough air to breathe. Thoughts of having these things can't help but put a smile on our faces. Being in complete contrast to when we complain, despite already having these blessings in our lives, complaining that somehow they are still not enough, we then consequently suffer. Which of course, as we are more aware of now, this stems from thinking that the things we have are not enough for us. Being more acquainted now of the power of our thoughts towards our emotions, isn't it that we now feel more conscious and are now more inclined towards being more responsible when it comes to our thoughts? That thoughts do not only cause physical manifestations to come about in our lives but as well as emotional manifestations. Knowing about this now, we are given the opportunity to be able to experiment and explore the vast plethora of emotions that we are capable of feeling as humans or simply as sentient beings. We can now mix and match certain emotions with specific thoughts allowing us the power to choose which emotions we would like to feel during a certain moment. This skill, at first, is going to be hard to master let alone control, especially if we only just have started realizing that we have such power or skill, but over time, like with everything else, constant practice allows us to become more proficient at it.

Lastly, let us now discuss the effects of our thoughts and emotions towards our actions. Actions like our emotions, also originate from our thoughts, moreover, at the same time, is also influenced by our feelings. As a simple example, whatever it is that we are doing now, is motivated by some specific idea that allows us to think that we should be doing it right now. As a concrete example, as I am writing this book, I am practically intoxicated by the idea that by all means, I should be writing this book right now, as of this very moment. I could be doing something else, but no, the main idea that is stuck in my mind right now is the idea of finishing this book. You, who is currently reading this book right now, is most likely compelled by some notion, that reading this book as of this moment is the best thing that you can do as of this moment. Perhaps supported by some sense that within this book you will find something significant, hence why you are reading it. With regards to emotions, which a lot of the time have been a compelling motivation towards our actions, you are reading right now because most possibly you may feel good about reading something right now, or perhaps looking at it from another perspective, you actually feel sad and so you read this book because somehow it makes you feel good. In that context, most of the time, we do the things that we do because they are the things that make us feel good or positive. Someone intentionally working towards feeling negative may be a bizarre phenomenon, but if in such case, the point is, whatever negative emotion that is that he or she wants to move forward to, the fact remains that he or she has willed to achieve such passion. If, in the case where one is unconsciously moving towards a certain negative feeling, then that is one of the main purposes of this book, for one to be made aware of such things – that indeed there will be times that we become unaware that we are causing ourselves to feel negative emotions, which has been mentioned and inevitably will be mentioned many more times in this book in many ways. Anyway, back to our actions is the results of our thoughts or emotions, one of our goals is to become highly aware of such fact consequently. At a certain point in our lives, such unawareness in this area may prove to be very unpleasant for us. The best example for this may come from actions that we do that originates from incessant thoughts and emotions of anger. How many times have we done something very destructive towards others and most especially towards ourselves just because we have acted out of fury? I know a lot of us here have done something very terrible only because we have let our anger take control of us and our actions. This perhaps is what we should be most wary of. As such, it is essential that we may be able to discern with pinpoint accuracy which thoughts and emotions are most beneficial for us. In little doses, it may prove to be unimportant, but overall, what becomes of our lives is ultimately the summation of all the thoughts that we have thought, emotions that we have felt, and actions that we have done.

That being said, as of this moment, whether you like or do not like wherever you are now, then it is most likely because of a particular thought, emotion, or action. Moreover, as we have been graciously pointing out, these things are within our control. If in the case that you do not like where you are now, then perhaps now is the time to take the time to be aware of whatever thought, emotion, or action, is driving you to be where you are now, for you to finally redirect yourself towards where you want to be, or more importantly who you want to be, and ultimately, how you want to be. At this point of the book, we have already discussed much of what we need to know to be able to do just that, much more so now that we are even more aware of the power of our actions, in relation to our emotions and our thoughts – specifically, following the positive thoughts and feelings that bring about highly satisfactory and fulfilling results. With that, let us now, with constant and unwavering awareness, move on to the next chapter.

Chapter 8

Overcome Your Past

Turning weaknesses into strengths

Society always hammers in our head from childhood to focus on our weaknesses (not that it's wrong) but it should also go along with focusing on your strengths as well. We spend our whole lives just dwelling on what we are not good at or lack that we forget to focus on what we excel at.

E.g., Zack is weak at math, but he writes excellent poetry and short stories. But his parents and teachers always tell him how bad he is at math and that he can't progress in life if he doesn't score well in math. He then gets disheartened thinking he can't do anything or that he's not smart enough and even stops writing poetry.

Accept your weaknesses

A lot of people in the pursuit of success are in this state of denial when it comes to their shortcomings, and in doing so, they end up failing more. There is no harm in accepting your shortcomings. It is not going to make you any lesser of a person in doing so.

Once you acknowledge your weakness, it will be easier for you to improve it or move past it. Accepting your weaknesses helps you to make more room for improvement and gives you a reason to grow more and expand your consciousness.

Get good enough at them

So let's go back to Zack's example, he was weak at math, but that does not mean he should also give up math completely and pursue his writing. He should take extra lessons and practice hard in math just enough to get a decent grade in it. Just because you have a weakness does not mean you have to let it stay a weakness forever. Conquer them if they are important to you. Just like in Zack's case because he had to pass the SATs.

Hire your weaknesses

Sometimes you got to hire people who are skilled in things you are not good at. It saves you time, effort and frustration. Nobody in this world is perfect at everything, and sometimes the best thing for you to do is to partner up with someone who is better at it. Synergizing to create a better result is the way to go!

Nobody is free from failure in this life. Your failures make or break you depending on what your perception is. You might have often seen successful people but never would have imagined what hardships or failures they had to go through to achieve that level of success. This is because it is impossible to have accomplished so much without ever experiencing failure.

Accept your failures

If you have failed in life no matter how big or small, accept them. There is no point staying in a state of denial or a sinking feeling of guilt and blame. Just remember, the only time you actually fail at something, is when you give up on that thing you are trying to do. This is something that you might want to try and remember every time you feel like giving up on something.

Failing is not being able to succeed in life. Deficiency is not being able to manage and not trying again or doing anything about it. It is simply planting the seeds of success.

Intrinsically, if we are going to decipher that emotion that we call "happiness," it is simply an emotion that correlates deeply with how we view our lives, and that is whether we do not have enough of the things that we need and want in life, or if we have more than enough. Of course, if we think that we have many of the things that we need and desire, then we become happy.

Being able to live in the moment, without fear, we find this amazing clarity that allows us to become impressively grateful within our lives. For having this clarity, unperturbed by fearful thoughts of the past and future, we can see that within the moment there is already so much to be thankful for. The air that we breathe in itself is something that we have to be highly grateful for. Something that perhaps we take so much for granted thinking it's only natural for us being able to breathe air. But think about it, there are so many planets present in our universe, or within our galaxy alone, but it is only Earth that has enough oxygen in the air for it to be capable of supporting life. The planet, moreover, is also something we can be thankful for. Think about it, releasing ourselves from thoughts of fear, and grounding ourselves to the present moment, everything as in everything we can find becomes something to be thankful for. Crazy as it may seem, but even our problems are worth being grateful for. Think about how without these problems, we wouldn't be able to grow and become better versions of ourselves. Realize that it is mainly because of these problems that have we learned to give ourselves more love and compassion.

Now, as we have discussed, suffering is simply the state of being in which we are directing our focus towards the things that we are losing during a certain moment. Gratitude is the exact opposite of that. Whenever we are thankful, isn't it that during that time we are thinking of something that we already have in our lives and feeling appreciative of it? Now, if we are going to analyze, during any moment, as long as we are alive, there is always, and I still mean, something to be thankful for.

Considering now that we have exercised meditation and have achieved self-control especially over our thoughts, we are now highly capable of choosing any specific idea within any moment. Which also means we are now even less bothered by unwanted thoughts that bring about negative responses from within us as the techniques we have learned allows us to skillfully redirect such negative thoughts into positive ones. That being so, we are then capable of directing our focus towards things that we can be thankful for. With this, we acquire the ability always to be thankful no matter what situation we are in.

Now, the most beautiful thing about gratitude is that it is a magnet for more things to be thankful for. The idea is that when we train our minds always to look for things to be grateful for, no matter what the situation is, then we'll still be able to find something to be grateful for. As we practice it more and more, it is like a muscle that also becomes more and more powerful. Unlike when we use our minds to always look for the negative in any situation, isn't it that we also always find something to be negative about? Thereby making us suffer. So which would we rather choose? Of course, we should rather be thankful. A lot of the time whenever we complain about a situation it's because we do it unconsciously. Also, we are not aware of the effects of complaining hence we go on complaining about things that do not go in our favor. Which ironically makes matters a lot worse than they are. Now, that we are aware of it, it would be much easier to get a hold of ourselves and stop this habit of complaining and redirect ourselves towards the right path of gratitude.

Gratitude is also the most effective way of making the things we value stay in our lives for the longest time possible. When we feel gratitude towards the things that we love, it is like we are creating an imaginary glue that binds us to them. The more that we feel gratitude and appreciation, the more that the things that we already have stick to us. To make this idea easier to visualize, let us again discuss the opposite of it. Whenever we complain about the things that we already have, isn't it that after some time these things somehow find a way to leave us? Especially with people, whenever we keep complaining about their presence in our life, isn't it that after some time they would eventually go? Simply because we did not appreciate them. Of course, anything or anyone that is not recognized, would not want to stay around us. For whenever we complain to people, it is very much like we are telling them that we do not want them in our life. As humans, one of our most basic needs is the need to be appreciated. Hence, whenever someone in our life does not feel appreciated, they would eventually leave so they could find someone else who would generously enjoy them. Which of course also works with material things. I've experienced many times having lost a material possession just because I did not understand it. The most concrete example is when we fail to take care of our material possessions, which is a way of saying that we do not value them, and so over time, not being well taken care of they eventually get broken. How many times have we regretted not being able to appreciate something that we had in our life only after when it's gone?

So we come back to appreciation or gratitude. In the most basic sense, feeling grateful towards the things that we value is our way of taking care of them, most especially our relationship with them. Going out of our way to let them know we appreciate them every day, our relationship with them strengthens and so, as we mentioned, they become attached to us as if they were glued to us. Consequently, we become more at peace and happy not just within ourselves but outside ourselves aswell. Speaking of which, in the first few chapters, we have been learning how to become appreciative of ourselves. Which again involves self-awareness, self-empathy, and self-love. When we are constantly self-aware, we are giving ourselves consistent attention, which much like appreciation is also a basic need. Doing these things we can create a very healthy relationship within ourselves consequently becoming our greatest source of peace and happiness. Our relationship with others is simply secondary. No matter how good our relationship is with those that are around us, in the end, as we have already been made aware of, our constant companion would be ourselves.

For us to be always appreciative towards ourselves is like always having a friend we can turn to for love and affection. Hence, being able to do so, we become the number one thing that we can always be thankful for no matter the situation. This way, being thankful all the time has become a constant possibility, for now, you can always say within yourself, "I am thankful I have me." With such a perspective, again, it doesn't matter if the world may crumble nor if the people you trust the most are not around. You are constantly able to rely on yourself even to your most basic of needs. Consequently, being able to do so, we are capable of appreciating even more then what we receive from another. Making us significantly more grateful, and it also can't be helped that we also become much happier.

Let failure free you

People are afraid of failing so much that they live all their lives worrying not to fail instead of focusing on the actual possibility of success. Allow yourself the margin to fail because if you go through it, it will set you free from all the fears and worries. It will make you stronger and move ahead on life easily.

Learn from them

Your failures and mistakes in life are not there to break you or to depress you. They are there to make you come out much stronger and help you to realize where all your strengths lie.

Make Plan B's and C's

Just because one way of reaching your goal didn't pan out the way you wanted it to, do not mean you give up and not try it any other way. Make another plan or a different strategy to achieve those goals. For example: if you can't afford to go to the college of your choice or didn't get hired from the company of which you wanted, then know that it is nothing personal against you and that you can find a better opportunity elsewhere.

Accept that certain things are not good for you

Sometimes life throws you a curveball and makes you realize things that didn't work out for you or you failed at were blessings in disguise. You then understand that you were meant to pursue other things that were better for you. Trust the universe and know that everything is always working in your favor.

Take responsibility for your life

Once you grow up and become an adult, you can no longer blame anyone for the problems in your life. Even if other people caused them, you can't give them the power to ruin your happiness. You should find ways to fix the problems in your life calmly and maturely instead of playing the blame game. Successful people always take 100% responsibility for their lives and so should you.

Embrace the pain

Don't run from failures or hurts in life because you are only setting yourself up for huge disappointments. Look them all in the eye and face them with courage because only then will the pain become lesser and be reduced down to nothing.

I hope now you can finally understand that failure is a part of life that should not only be accepted but to be openly talked about. Failure shouldn't be people don't think of it as something shameful to discuss. Who knows you could be an inspiration to someone later on?

Chapter 9

PHYSIOLOGY OF SELF-COMPASSION

As we see now, much of the things that affect us can be found internally, not externally. Specifically, our thoughts. Hence, now, the importance of being able to classify the role of our minds in our lives. If we would analyze, as we have been discussing in the past chapters, our thoughts are basically what influences us most during any situation. Which leads us to the conclusion that if we can take control of our thoughts, then we are also able to take control of our composure or our emotions. If we observe further, it is primarily because of our lack of control over our minds that we can experience a lot of negative emotions. Whenever we let our minds take control and bombard us with negative thoughts, we become crippled. Every time we allow it to do so means we consciously forget that we are the ones that should be in control. We are surrendering ourselves to our weaknesses. The mind is practically the filter we use as to what we're going to choose to allow what comes into our lives. Whether we're going to subscribe to thoughts infested with fear or thoughts charged with love. So, much of what we need to do is being able to have self-control enough to be able to direct the ideas that we wish to have. To remember that the mind is our servant and we are the master, not the other way around. To be able to realize that we have such power is our goal. Whenever we let our thoughts take control, it is simply because we have forgotten that we are in control. We have surrendered to our minds the authority to navigate our ships, when in fact it is only a tool that we use to navigate through life. In a sense, our thoughts are the satellite that we use to receive and send the signals we wish to convey. That is simply it. We must be able to reaffirm this within ourselves.

To further understand and enlighten ourselves with the role of our minds in our lives, let us review everything we have discussed. To start with, when it comes to choosing our self-identity, isn't it that it is our thoughts or ideas about who we are that influences it in the first place? Hence our self-identity is programmed through our minds. Using our awareness, we can choose to direct our minds to accept a certain idea over another. So, if we are choosing between the concept of the body and the concept of the soul as a foundation for our sense being, we have to do so through our minds. That being so if we are unaware of this, our mind, without our permission, automatically chooses this for us. Which means, our brain takes the role of the leader whenever we let unawareness govern us.

Further accentuating on the importance of having awareness in our lives. If we mindlessly let our minds decide for us, we become a stranger even to ourselves. The thought, in a way, is the vice-captain who assumes responsibility for ourselves whenever we fail to become responsible for our ship.

And whether we have a hateful, inconsiderate, unforgiving, and fearful vice-captain, or a self-loving, self-compassionate, forgiving, courageous one of course entirely depends on our supervision. Now being aware of the consequences of letting our minds get the best of us. Let us now figure out a way for us to reclaim control over our thoughts and ultimately over the entirety of our lives, and that is through meditation. A lot of people may have different descriptions as well as methods as to how it should be done, but the simplest way around the concept of meditation is plainly to cultivate awareness. And the easiest way for someone to do that is to simply become aware of the most fundamental process that connects us to life.

Now, our main focus of this chapter is to accentuate the fact that breathing consciously promotes and cultivates our awareness. Perhaps this is not the first book related to meditation that you have read; then this will not be the first time that you've heard such information. Think of it this way, oxygen from the air we breathe is practically the fuel that we use to operate our minds. Maybe you are thinking, what about the food we eat? Well, let's say the food that we ingest is more for our body, not our minds. Moving on, the more oxygen that we inhale, the more aware we become, hence improving our chances at achieving control over ourselves, especially our thoughts. From the term itself, "conscious breathing," it is urgently suggested that we become more conscious and to put more attention to our breathing. Most of the time, if you haven't noticed it yet, something that also went unnoticed by me for years, or something I haven't given importance to until I was made aware of it, is the fact that we do breathe mechanically. Breathing being an involuntary action, it continues to go on even if we are not conscious of it. Thereby, actively involving one's self in breath, we became more aware and grounded to what is happening to us intrinsically. This gives us more capacity to catch and stop ourselves whenever we are thinking about a certain negative thought which could potentially become the cause to us transitioning into an unfavorable mood. Also, consciously breathing, we learn to detach ourselves from the ideas we are thinking, due to this, we can create space between our awareness and our beliefs. Doing so, we become significantly much more effective at stopping and redirecting our thoughts and our consciousness.

Meditation as well grounds us into the present which allows us to see and be aware of the things that are already available to us. Being present connects us to the abundance that is already within our grasp, which are already available to us. Being compared to the present, we are most connected to reality. We can appreciate readily the real blessings that we already have. The oxygen that we breathe in itself is already very much a blessing for us. Which is one of the most symbolic things that we may relate to meditation? Meditation being an activity that improves our connection with our breath, with the oxygen that we inhale, it signifies our deep relationship with life in itself. Breathing consciously, we exercise our most basic right of control. Doing so, we also allow space for silence to be cultivated within our thoughts. Which is the most important thing that meditation does for us. As this silence becomes the reference point for us to be able to achieve higher degrees of mindfulness. And it is exactly through this space of silence that we can contemplate on the many things regarding our self-awareness, our self-identity, and practically everything that we have discussed and are going to talk about in this book.

As we have mentioned in a previous part of this book, we are going to need lots of time to contemplate and reflect on the things we need to figure out. Meditating regularly helps us speed up that process. Imagine, as we consciously breathe in and breathe out, we also become increasingly conscious of not just our breathing but also everything that happens around us and within us, of course, our thoughts included. As we consciously breathe, our focus dwells mainly on the act of observation hence making us very sensitive and alert, therefore, during this state, we get to watch over our thoughts with much greater ease. It would be as if we are watching a movie, as we are letting our thoughts drift through in the right in front of us, with us simply observing these thoughts that arises and passes through. This way, we simply become a watcher of our thoughts, and through this, we cultivate our awareness of our thoughts, and from this space of knowledge, we are then going to be more successful at catching ourselves thinking of an undesirable impression. Which, of course, being highly sensitive and alert to the ideas that come and go, consequently we become more capable of redirecting them when needed. From this space of awareness, as we breathe in and out all the more consciously, we are going to be able to contemplate and ruminate through our thoughts from a more relaxed state of being. And as we practice more and more, we find it a lot easier to do so. Giving us more control over our thoughts, and gradually over our emotions, and so forth. We become infinitely more calm and composed and in control of ourselves. Our minds are no longer left unsupervised as we are now more in control of ourselves and so we become more inclined towards peace. Which is the truest standard of a rational being?

Speaking of rationality, now let us also discuss meditation as a method of surrender. For the first part of this chapter, we discussed how meditation and conscious breathing, achieves for us a much higher quality of central control or self-discipline. This time we are going to explain how reflection can be used to do the opposite, but this time regarding our control of the outside world. How many times have we frustrated ourselves or struggled profusely over just because of the actions of the people or the world around us? A lot of times, or maybe even every single day of our lives, isn't it? Although, yes, we have also had our glorious moments regarding events related to people or situations pleasing us, overall, certain people or events will always find its way into displeasing us, no matter what we do. Unless of course, we do not care what other people do or what happens around us. We surrender to the fact that people or situations will always manage to arouse a negative response from us which consequently is what makes it lose its power over us. Simply because when we surrender to such fact, we let go of our idea of control towards people and situations. Which is the main reason why we get frustrated over people or situations not following what we want? We take it against them for not supporting what we want. Which is impossible. Perhaps up to a certain extent, we can control people or situations, but this will never be so for all the time. People in positions of higher authority or power have a harder time accepting this fact because they are more used to being in control. Which is also what makes them significantly more frustrated whenever things do not go their way. Hence, the simplest solution, to surrender, to let go, not everything is within our control. Thus, for this, we must utilize meditation. Whenever we are faced with difficult people or events, always the best thing to do is to take a deep breath, first to be fully conscious of ourselves, and secondly for us to be able to remain calm. Being able to act composed during such times, is always the best thing we can do to achieve the most favorable outcome. How many times have we let our emotions or actions run rampant during extremely difficult situations that instead of being able to find resolve we find that we made the situation worse than when it started?

Hence, we come back to the idea of self-control. In the end, it is only ourselves that we are truly in control of. To fantasize with the idea of being in control of people or situations is completely irrational. We have to accept the fact that we are never going to have full control over external things. If that is so then, we wouldn't have to go through any problem in life, which would make it kind of boring. Experience is not designed that way. Hence, we have foreshadowed that being able to surrender is an act of rationality. Although we surrender our power for external control, it is highly compensated as we generate and direct all our focus towards being able to control ourselves. This way, we will never get frustrated considering that if we have achieved a high level of control over ourselves, then we will not only be in control over our actions but also our thoughts and emotions. Hence, we acquire the capability to always be calm and composed during any situation or any difficult person we may face in our life. Which becomes the ultimate foundation to which we are going to base our peace from. Paradoxically, the act of letting go is the highest act of control. Letting go of control as the truest manifestation of power. This is what we achieve through meditation, through constant practice of conscious breathing, through consistent persistency to cultivate awareness. Our fate handed to us in the palm of our hands, one of the highest forms of self-fulfillment one can achieve in a lifetime.

What is a positive mind?

Did you know that all things in this universe including thoughts are energy particles? If you think positively, the world will match your energy and ideas by bringing you a positive outcome. Therefore, it is very important for you never to fall prey to the negative spiral and self-doubting thoughts your mind tends to create. Because whatever you think in life usually becomes your self-fulfilling prophecy.

A positive mind always thinks and visualizes about the best possible outcome for any situation, while a negative mind sinks only in misery and despair. The following story is ideal for explaining this:

The two wolves within

There is a story about an old man who teaches his little grandson a very important lesson in life.

He asked his grandson, "There are two wolves within all of us, and they are always at battle with each other. One wolf represents all the good things in life such as joy, kindness, compassion, love, truth, and hope. Whereas the other one is anger, evil, hate, lies, and hopelessness. Which wolf do you think wins?"

Confused, the child replies, "I don't know grandfather, which one wins?"

His grandfather wisely smiles at him and gives him the most important lesson of his life. One that would build and shape his character forever.

"The one that you feed son."

This story applies to our mindsets. If we feed our minds positivity, then we can conquer the highest mountains in life. But if we supply our dark side, then we will never be able to reach anywhere in life.

Conditioned minds

It's not always your fault if you end up having a negative mindset. Society, parents, friends and the media all play their role towards that. You get told every day that something is impossible to achieve or attain and you end up thinking that for the rest of your life. It is your responsibility to break off these shackles that bind you to conformity and mediocrity.

The power of the subconscious mind

Your mind is divided into two portions: the conscious and the subconscious. While we are only aware of what our thoughts and feelings are when we are awake, the subconscious mind is working 24/7 and absorbing everything. When psychologists try to help people with their limiting beliefs, they are always trying to tap into the account on the subconscious level.

The sub-conscious mind is very powerful, and in fact, controls the conscious mind on the surface. All our deepest thoughts, feelings, desires and fears reside here. Therefore, even if you consciously try to suppress a thought or emotion, know that it stems from the subconscious, and it is not going to go away until you address it and try to resolve it.

The subconscious mind never stops working, and you find answers to all of your problems by tapping in its potential. The subconscious mind is very strong, and you can't alter its thinking by simply using willpower. It is the part of the brain that controls your conscious, so whatever feelings or thoughts that you are experiencing now, chances are they are stemming from your subconscious.

Whatever you experience on a conscious level gets recorded in the subconscious mind even if you don't remember it.

To change your mindset, you need to go to the core and start taking care of your subconscious mind because it also controls the body. This is why many people develop illnesses because they have stress and anxiety. Constantly thinking about negative events or experiences affects the body in various ways.

If you nurture your mind (both consciously and subconsciously), you will see a positive result in your life. You will heal easily, your mood will be better, and you will attract other positive things in your life.

Suffering is a state of mind, no more no less. Specifically, one that involves thinking that we are losing something as of the moment. Missing something in the sense that we are focused on what we do not have, instead of what we do have in life. A behavior that is highly connected to our natural tendency for survival, or more commonly known as our survival instinct. Of course, as a defense mechanism to anything that potentially endangers our well-being. Which, as we can see, has got a lot to do with declining resources. Resources which can come down to the most necessities in life; food, water, and air. Imagine, for example, a man trapped in a cave, gradually losing air to breathe, heavily panicking as he notices his body and mind slowly getting weaker because of the lack of oxygen circulating in his system. Panicking, as a definite reminder that without air to breathe, he is inevitably going to die, and so, he suffers. But apart from our basic needs, we also have higher requirements. Which also translates to our needs which is beyond our physical needs. For having nourished the body, we then look for things that feed our soul, our emotions. For example, our fascination with listening to music. We look for music knowing that it inspires a pleasant passion within us.

Suffering then has also got a lot to do with our desires. Contemplating on the fact that these resources that we need in life are things that we desire for ourselves. Considering their importance to our overall well-being, we cannot help but want these things whether or not they are truly a necessity in our lives as long as we get a certain kind of satisfaction from whatever it is that we desire. Of course, we cannot be afraid of losing something that we do not want in the first place. We cannot grieve over something that we do not value. Isn't it that we could care less over losing something that we do not appreciate in the first place?

But this instinct of ours does not necessarily need to invoke suffering. We suffer because we hold on to what our intuition tells us. We linger on to the thought that we are losing something when all we have to do is to view it as a guide. Our instinct may say that we are missing something, but that doesn't mean we should react to it in an overwhelmingly negative manner, such as panicking for example. Instead, we can be thankful that we are aware. For simply being aware of a negative situation, we are then capable of counteracting the situation by finding ways on how to prevent it from getting worse.

Going back to our self-identification. If we are identified with our bodies, certain events would have profound effects towards us. Such as losing material things. But if we are identified simply with our awareness, amazingly, many events in life that would seem devastating to most would seem trivial to us. Since, our personalities being rooted in our awareness, our desires also are greatly reduced, or in another sense, we become significantly detached from our desires. Because as awareness, simply being alive or aware is already a lot for us. As awareness, it doesn't take a lot for us to become fully satisfied, and so we are incredibly low-maintenance beings. Being identified as awareness then, there is much little motivation to suffer. As opposed to being identified with the body, we have to have so many materialistic things just for us to be satisfied, and so we become high-maintenance beings. For this, we can suffer greatly.

Suffering then involves a state of being in which we are too attached or too identified with the things that we are or the things that we have. Being greatly attached to these things, we react with a lot of displeasure even at the mere possibility of losing them. So, we must not hold on to these things so desperately or else we are indeed going to suffer. We must learn then how to take all things lightly, more so as an act of self-love and self-compassion. We acknowledge for suffering for what it is and then we can let go of it. Looking back on the things that we have discussed so far, our suffering particularly stems from our attachment towards negative thoughts such as hate. Hence the importance of all that we have discussed up to this point. Such as our self-identity, self-awareness, self-love, and forgiveness. These things point towards the things that we want and need in life, as well as the things we do not want and need. And these things that we do not want and need, to simplify, are those things that make us suffer.

So with all that so far, what we have discussed, is the fact suffering is not entirely caused by the situations that are happening to us, but more so the thinking that we have during these situations. Articulating pain in this manner, we find in ourselves a much greater understanding on how we are going to avoid and more so completely rid ourselves of it. Which is of course to change our thinking about a certain situation. To give a good example, think of the times that we are complaining about a certain event in our life. Let's say, we are complaining about how our bills become more and more expensive. When we are doing so, we are focusing on the idea that we are losing more money because our laws are becoming more expensive. Hence, we suffer. But instead, if we were to think that thankfully we have a job, and we have our gifts and talents that we may use so that we may be able to acquire the money that we need to pay these ever increasing bills, then we become more positive about the situation. When we focus on what we lose, indeed we miss, but if we focus on what we have, we thereby gain more of these things.

In this way, suffering then becomes a choice. We either focus on what makes us hurt or on what makes us not hurt. That ultimately, getting ourselves out of suffering is our responsibility, and is most definitely within our power. A lot of times we think that we are helpless towards these situations, but that can be no further from the truth. One of the noblest goals of this book is to slowly but surely give you back that power, and if you have already done so, strengthen that power even more. Which is what we have been nurturing so far. As we are becoming more self-aware, more self-compassionate, and more forgiving, we gradually acquire more power to have more self-control and inclination towards less suffering. For as we have declared, what we want most is to have more and more peace which in its most ideal sense also means virtually less and less suffering. With this thought, having learned about the mechanics of pain, we are more capable of doing so. Peace, we are learning now, is more a matter of choice, a matter of deciding that we do not want to suffer.

The Way to a Positive Mindset

Self-Acceptance

The first step to a healthy and positive mindset is to accept yourself no matter what. It doesn't matter what your skin color, weight or gender is because you are not a tiny little box that someone ticks based on the demographic you belong to. You are much more than that. You have the power to move mountains in life, yet like most people, you end up struggling with just tiny hills. So don't let your insecurity whatever it maybe hold you back from doing anything in life.

Love and accept every part of yourself and project it onto the world so that you get the same in return. Treat yourself kindly before anyone else does.

Practice Affirmations

This is a really important part of the process. Affirmations are statements, and declarations one says thinks or writes about oneself, to train the mind to think positively.

Once we start believing it, our subconscious mind is going to absorb it as well.

Positive affirmations are instrumental in developing a more confident and strong mind. You use them every day in different forms so that they get embedded deep within your account.

Start by saying a few positive things about yourself and your life. You can either say it in front of a mirror or write it down in a journal. Whatever works for you as long as you do it every day.

E.g., you can say "I have an amazing life, and I can do whatever I want."

"I am beautiful, and I have a lovely body."

"I love my family and friends."

These are just examples, and of course, you can customize your affirmations to what you would prefer. You can write positive quotes and stick them on your workstation or mirror as well so that your mind reads it every day and eventually accepts it. We become what we think about.

Positive affirmations help you attract all the things that you mention in them easily. This is also just like the Law of Attraction.

Practice Gratitude

Another crucial element of a positive mind is gratitude. You need to be thankful for all the things that you have been blessed with in life. These could be from the very little and mundane to the big and complex things in life. Everything happens for a reason. The pain that you see today will be the blessing you see tomorrow.

That break-up you are heartbroken about is preparing you for a better love life with another loving and caring person. Getting fired from a job may be a sign that you have a better career opportunity out there for you.

That illness you might have is here to tell you to value your health and help others who are struggling with the same disease. Our response to whatever happens to us is the final result of the experience we have in our life. So, in essence, there are no failures, just our actions or thoughts towards whatever happens to us.

We all have our battles and demons to fight with. They are not here to defeat us but to make us stronger and braver. It's hard but you have to be grateful and only then will you see positive things manifest into your life that you could never have imagined.

Surround yourself with positive people

One of the most important things that you can do is to interact more with positive people. Building a support system which encourages you is vital in helping you achieve your goals and ambitions. Avoid engaging with toxic or negative people who'll only bring you down.

If you want to make better friendships, then join different clubs or meet-up groups and build new connections with like-minded people.

Studies show that people who have an active and healthy social life tend to neither get less sick nor suffer from feelings of depression. The sense of isolation is very frustrating, but try to always have some good friends or like minded people around you that you can interact with on a regular basis.

Be aware of your thoughts

Most of the time people have their ideas running on default, and they are not mindful of them. This means that there is no filter to stop any negative thoughts and so it is really easy for them to fall prey to the vicious cycle of negativity. It might seem quite difficult to put a filter on your thoughts, but with a little practice, you can become more of a conscious person when thinking about things. This is not to say to stop or suppress your thoughts because that is almost impossible. But to change the way you feel about things when you see or experience them.

See the positive in everything

You don't have to be a Pollyanna and pretend to be happy when life is difficult. But your response should be towards tackling every situation and doing something about it. Only then will things start improving and changing the course of their direction.

This also includes seeing the good in others as well. Try to see the product in everyone because this will prevent you from having any negative biases or perceptions about others. Compliment others because who knows you might end up making someone else's day wonderful.

Spread positivity around

The best way to be more positive is to cover it around others as well.

Smile — research shows that smiling makes the brain release endorphins and serotonin that help relax the body and mind. Smiling is infectious as well, and you will notice a positive response 99% of the time whenever you smile at someone.

Do volunteer work — helping the less fortunate will make you count your blessings in life and be more grateful.

Play with children and pets — they are the most innocent beings that you can easily make happy. You will appreciate the little joys in life that come from playing with them.

Donate — give away things you don't need to people who do. It could be old clothes, books or even money.

Meditate

Meditation has been proven to reduce stress and anxiety from people's life. You don't necessarily have to join a yoga class to be good at meditating. You can meditate in a quiet room in as little as 10 minutes a day. Just set some time aside for yourself and clear your mind of all the clutter and worries that make you feel all anxious or angry.

Breathe deeply and close your eyes. Focus on just being relaxed and happy. Once you start doing this regularly, you can even increase the time of your meditation, and it won't seem uncomfortable or strange to you anymore.

No more surviving, it's time for thriving!

Whatever you have experienced in life, it is time to move past it and stop using the victim card. Positive people even if they are victims to circumstances, don't just sit there and blame others or life for their misery.

You can change your life if you just put your mind to it, but it will only happen if you stop carrying around the baggage of victimhood and self-pity. As harsh as it sounds, nobody likes a pity party. People might feel bad for you for one day and try to help you, but if all they see is you wallowing all the time and not do anything about it, they will start avoiding you and not feel bad for you anymore. Be an inspiration to others by thriving at life and not just surviving.

Forgive others

The last step to having a positive mindset is to forgive people for their mistakes because nobody is perfect. Holding on to anger and resentment for what you experienced in the past burdens you forever. You end up walking around with so much pain and anger that it is impossible for you to have a peace of mind. At the end of the day forgiving someone is more about the sanity of your mind so forgive people and move on.

Having a positive mind is not that difficult once you move past these barriers that block you. It is also not possible to never be negative. The key is to maintain a healthy balance that is gravitating mostly towards the positive side.

Forgiving others does not mean that you are ok with what they did to you nor are you condoning any of their actions. It is simply another process of healing from the hurt you are going through. Most of the times people can't progress with their lives is because they haven't forgiven the people who wronged them.

Forgiveness also makes you a better person and helps you to be a more compassionate person. Even if the person didn't ask for forgiveness, but you have to forgive for your sake.

Chapter 10

Putting Yourself Into Action

One easy way to increase your self-love and your standard of living is by lavishing love and care on yourself. Taking adequate care of yourself, both physically and psychologically, will help you look and feel better, which will increase your self-love.

Here are some examples of how to take care of yourself:

1: Never miss your night sleep for anything

Always ensure you get adequate sleep. Sometimes you may be tempted to stay up, attend to certain issues, and catch up with rest the next day. In as much as you can make up for the sleepless night, nothing compares to that good night sleep you missed.

The human body secretes hormones that signal the brain to shut down and rest during the night. Getting adequate sleep is a good way to improve your quality of life. This usually leads to an all-around healthier life which you can benefit from.

2: Engage in physical exercises

Physical exercise helps keep your body healthy enough to serve you better. You can start with maybe joining a local gym, start cycling, taking part in a sport, taking regular long walks or maybe jogging. Exercise usually helps people clear their mind and feel good about themselves due to a sense of motivation and achievement.

In addition to ensuring that you stay fit and healthy, engaging in physical exercise can do so many things for you. Coupled with a good weight-management diet plan, physical activities are one of the surest ways to lose weight and keep away the unwanted weight.

3: Mind what you eat

This piece of advice is one most of us do not want to hear. Most of us want to eat whatever catches our fancy and whatever we crave. It has always been said that we become what we eat.

If there is one thing that ensures you to live a good life for as long as you live, it is an insistence on nothing but natural organic, clean foods and avoiding processed junk. Eating good can usually have a positive effect on you, making you feel good about yourself and life in general.

There are several ways you can give yourself special treats similar to those you would give to someone you love. Here are methods of treating yourself

Occasionally pamper yourself

Pampering yourself involves taking time off everything that keeps you busy so you can concentrate on giving yourself some special treatments such as a sensual massage or visiting a spa center.

When it comes to increasing self-love, how you pamper and treat yourself can help improve how you see and how you feel about yourself as a whole.

When you do well, reward yourself

One easy way to develop self-love is to pay yourself whenever you achieve a milestone. Paying yourself helps you feel better and makes you want to succeed more and to prove to yourself that you have all it takes to reach.

Set regular targets and decide what incentives and rewards you will give yourself each time you successfully achieve your goal. Your goal can range from cultivating a new habit of starting something you have been putting off for ages such as taking piano lessons, writing a new book, starting that small business, etc.

Whenever you achieve that feat, reward yourself by buying yourself that gift you want, taking yourself out to somewhere cool and fun to give yourself a special treat, or hang out with that special someone who makes you feel like you have no care in the world.

It may not be easy to develop self-love if you do not change certain things about yourself that reduce your self-worth and self-respect. Certain factors can make you feel unworthy of anything.

When you change certain things about yourself, things that affect your self-esteem and how you see yourself, you will increase your self-love.

Here are some tips on things you can change in your life and increase self-love:

Simplify your life

Many of us complicate things for ourselves by clustering our lives with things we can easily do without. When you take up more things than you can easily handle within the time and space available to you, you end up with several unfinished tasks and abandoned projects. The more you begin things and never finish them, and the more you leave things here and there half done, the more your self-confidence and self-respect decrease.

When you simplify your life by ensuring you take up only things you can easily handle, life becomes easier and more interesting since you have more time to focus on yourself and other very important issues in your life such as your family and relationship. The more time you have to concentrate on the things that matter, the more you love the person you are.

But, how can you simplify your life? Here are some ideas:

Review your circle of friends

Let us be truthful, some people in your circle of friends should not be there. Certain people that occupy space in your life never make any meaningful contribution from year to year. Instead, such people are negative, never seem to encourage you and make you feel bad at yourself.

Evaluate your friends and decide which ones to keep and which ones to start spending less time with. People that cause you to do things that result in self-loathing should not be on your friend's list. It is important to understand that to live a quality life; you do not need many friends at all. All you need is a handful that can bring out the best in you, help you overcome your negative habits, learn new positive practices, and believe in yourself and your ability to achieve all your goals.

Review your To-Do list

Several things on your daily To-Do list are things you can delete and not feel as if anything vital is missing from the list. Evaluate the activities you engage in, and you spend a lot of time doing without getting many results and get rid of them. Consider the sitcoms and soap operas you spend hours watching at home and see how you can reduce the number of hours you spend watching them.

You need to understand that anything that does not help you get better will not increase your self-love and progression in life, therefore should not be a part of your life.

The fewer things you have to attend to, the more time you have to do things that improve your life and benefit you as a person, things such as learning new skills, reading new books and joining new causes.

Become a Minimalist

Minimalism is all about living with less and still feeling fulfilled. Becoming a minimalist entails reducing the amount of stuff you have in places such as your home or office, such as your clothing, papers, books, electronics, etc. Minimalism can also involve moving from a big home to a smaller one.

A smaller home means you have to live with fewer belongings that require less time and resources to maintain. The extra time you would have spent keeping a big home is the time you can use to pursue other things that can improve your life.

Self-Compassion & Relationships

The importance of relations in everybody's life cannot be denied. The human relationships and social structure is quite impressive and distinguishes us from other species. A relation can be with your relatives, guy friend or a girlfriend. It is good to maintain a healthy relationship with people close to you to gain trust and acceptance. In healthy relationships you are not isolated, you can share your views and thoughts and ask for advice. Apart from this the quality of relationships that you have with others also affects our physical and mental health.

Like its effects on other spheres of life, self-compassion, relations and the personal life of the person are also interlinked. Self-compassionate people are more happy, caring, supportive and accepting in their relations. Such people grant more autonomy and freedom to their partners and close ones. They have the tendency to share their perspective, thought, and ideas with their close ones. Such people also lead a good life, because they can share the happenings in their lives and release off some burden.

Relationships are affected greatly by even small acts of compassion. Self-compassion and compassion with others give us more personal control, loving nature, and confidence. When we have control over ourselves, we know about our limits and our abilities, and we work and cooperate with others according to our capacities. Loving nature is equally important in any relation. It can make us supportive and caring towards other people in our lives. Confidence is also something which matters the most in relations; if you want to have perfect communication and understanding with others, confidence might be the right key.

Lack of self-compassion can lead a person to rejection sensitivity in their relationships. As described earlier rejection sensitivity in relationships is often a problem that needs to be addressed either on your own or by consulting a specialist before it is too late. The rejection sensitive people lead a problematic life, and they usually perceive and think negatively about the outcome of their relations. The chances of such people to engage in constructive communication are very less. Apart from this, they might self-silence themselves. Self-silencing might help such people momentarily in escaping from the realities, but eventually, the negative outcomes will start to appear in your relationships. The way out from the problem of rejection sensitivity is to practice self-compassion, to get rid of their complexes.

Self-compassion and compassion are also helpful in romantic relationships. Two people who display self-compassion for themselves almost automatically generate compassion for the other spouse because of their optimism and space they provide for their other partner in every aspect of life. They do not employ criticism or rudeness or being biased for solving their problems, they are calm, and as the communication gap in them is a lot smaller they are able to solve their matters with harmony. In this way, they make better spouses than people who show little or no compassion.

Professional relations with customers, other organizations and among the staff itself are also important. It has been noted that people who regularly receive and practice compassion while at work; voluntarily or involuntarily, have a good response to their tasks and their capacities are enhanced. They see their organization, their colleagues and themselves in a positive light. They feel positive emotions like contentment and joy. Moreover, their commitment to their job is noteworthy.

There is no surprise in the fact that people who make use of self-compassion are the ones who have compassion for other people in their lives. Compassionate type of people instead of ignoring the sufferings of others, tend to notice and acknowledge them and then try their best to alleviate their pain with warmth, kindness, and understanding. They do not consider the physical, monetary or social situation of the affected fellow; rather they try to recognize what they have in common with them. Moreover, according to experts to get an idea of what self-compassion is like, it is quite helpful to see compassion in other people around you. So the compassionate people can lead the way by setting an example of compassion for others to follow.

Maintaining Self Compassion

After having a thorough look at the benefits of self-compassion, our major concern now is maintaining it. At first, being self-compassionate might take some courage and seem unnatural. Some individuals might find it difficult, especially people who have recently experienced trauma, so in some cases to get a kick start you may need some sort of psychologist or a therapist, who might help you begin from somewhere. The strategies discussed in this chapter will considerably help you in maintaining self-compassion.

Consider How You Would Treat Someone Else

This actually might be the simplest solution to maintain self-compassion. Imagine that someone close to you got rejected or failed and came to you. How would you treat that person? What are the words that you would say? Which words would you not like to say to them? Certainly, you will take the initiative to encourage or motivate them, so that they can overcome their problems and start their normal life. Similarly, it is quite effective in maintaining self-compassion when you treat your-self in the same way as you treat your close ones.

Take a look at you language before you finished this book, you might have been in the habit of criticizing yourself without realizing it. So it might be quite useful to pay attention to the words that you speak to your-self in or after difficult situations. Try not to say something to yourself which you would not like to say to someone beloved, if you are doing otherwise then certainly it should be termed as self-criticism and it is well established that self-criticism is a major hindrance in your path to success.

Comforting Oneself with Physical Gestures

It is a well-known fact that kind, and caring gestures have a quick effect on our operating abilities and our body itself. Such positive gestures activate your soothing parasympathetic system. In some cultures, it is said that kind and caring gestures toward oneself drop you in your body from your head, because the head does not want to stick with the storyline and loves to deny realities because of the human instinct. While the body stands for the place where you get comfort, and you are away from emotion. In this regard, any gesture can work, but the gestures of putting your hand on your heart and holding your arm, patting on your shoulder or massaging your temples are quite effective.

Memorizing Compassionate Phrases

The maintenance of self-compassion in the time of adversities might seem to be a challenge, but you can take deep breaths, gently put one of your hands on your heart and repeat the phrases below:

- ❖ This is a moment of suffering
- ❖ Suffering is a part of life
- ❖ May I be kind to myself
- ❖ May I give myself the compassion I need

These phrases include the essence of all the three discussed components of self-compassion that have been described in chapter 1. The first phrase gives the message of being mindful of the sufferings. The second phrase tells us that all human beings have to go through sufferings, so there is nothing to be ashamed of when you are in trouble. The third phrase compels us to leave self-criticism and hold fast to self-compassion. The last phrase gives us the message that our self is in dire need of self-compassion, so we deserve it the most in the situation of adversity. This practice is a sort of meditation, and it is observed that talking to oneself or doing meditation at times can be effective in controlling emotions and being rational.

Self-compassion Diary

Try to keep a self-compassion diary for a period you like. Writing a diary can help you in expressing your own emotions to yourself, and it contributes to well-being both emotionally and physically. Write about the things that made you feel sad, ashamed or stressed. As you are writing, don't try to be judgmental of your experiences. In the end, write some words in a reassuring tone that might comfort you. At the end of the day read it again. Keeping a diary will surely help you in organizing your thoughts and translate them for compassion towards yourself.

Morning Rituals

Try to make it a habit of doing a morning ritual every day. Consider yourself fortunate that you have woken up and you are alive and breathing. Reflect on the importance of your life and commit yourself, that you will not waste it and try the best to develop yourself and expand your feeling not only to yourself but also others around you. Surely you can add more thoughts to the ritual that you are going to practice. This will automatically help you be more self-compassionate towards yourself throughout the day, and its effects on compassion towards others will also be noteworthy.

Practice Acts of Kindness

Now if you have practiced all this, you would certainly love to enjoy everyday acts of kindness towards yourself and the people around you. If you see yourself in some distress show some empathy towards yourself if someone else is suffering try to solve their problem and make them happy. Even if someone has hurt you a bit which affected you, and you have them in mind, try to forgive that person and look forward to having a good relationship with them. Ultimately all of this would help you in your aim of developing self-compassion, because when we have compassion for others, we get to know their situation and what they might be thinking and what do they want. Similarly, when you are having problems, you would also do the same for yourself.

Self-compassion through Writing

Writing can also help you in your efforts for self-compassion. The writing exercise can be broken down into three parts:

- ❖ Ponder over the imperfections that make you feel down.
- ❖ From the viewpoint of a loving friend, write a supposed letter to yourself.
- ❖ Feel the compassion comforting and soothing you.

Everyone is not perfect and has imperfections that make them feel insecure, feeling of shame and inadequacy. In the first step write about the issues that give you a feeling of inadequacy. What are the emotions that surface when you think about those issues? Try to feel your emotions and then write them down in words.

In the second step think about a best friend of yours who knows all your weaknesses and strengths, including the issues that you wrote earlier. Ponder over what you think your friend might think of you, and how that friend loves you with all your shortcomings and imperfections. This friend knows the limits of the nature of humans and is quite forgiving towards you. Now try writing a letter to yourself from the viewpoint of that good friend and try to focus on what that friend will tell you in the moment of despair, and how they would convey the compassion that they feel towards you. Also, think of possible suggestions your friend would give to you.

After writing the letter put it aside for a while and rest for a few minutes. Now read it again and enjoy the comfort it gives to you in the form of compassion.

You would feel the compassion being showered on you.

Conclusion

One thing you need to pay attention to, something that will help you love yourself more and treat yourself with greater respect, is your level of confidence. Self-confidence is one attribute that makes you daring enough to believe you can succeed where and when everyone thinks you will surely fail.

Have you seen a smaller boxer taking on an bigger opponent and winning the contest and wondered what gave him the guts to challenge the giant? Only self-confidence borne of self-belief and respect can drive a man to challenge what is greater than he is and come out victorious.

How can you grow your level of self-confidence so you can dare more, win more, love yourself more, and live more?

Here are some ideas to help you:

Go places you have always avoided

Fear is the major reason why you have a low level of confidence or lack self-confidence entirely. The best way to conquer you fear to do the very thing you fear. To do this, come up with a list of things you fear, and rate them 1 to 10 with one being less fearful, and ten being most fearful. Start doing the things you fear beginning with the ones, you fear less. As you tackle what you don't fear most, you will grow confidence to deal with the things you fear the most, and after time, you will be amazed that you are overcoming doing the things you never thought you could do.

Whenever you attempt something scary and succeed, you naturally raise the love, respect, and belief you have in yourself.

For example, if you fear public speaking, you will always feel inferior because you cannot speak out when and where most of your peers are speaking.

However, the day you learn to dare that fear and damn the consequences, you will notice an improvement in how you see yourself, which will help you dare more, achieve more, love the new more daring you, and live a better life.

Take up challenging tasks

If you keep taking tasks that are within your qualification and expertise, you may not be able to build the right level of self-confidence needed to attain your dreams. Sometimes you need to defy all odds and attempt the things everyone says are impossible. You may not achieve success on every venture you set out to achieve, but you will at least become more fearless and courageous to try other such things in the future.

The more you build your courage, the more you develop self-love. The more self-love you develop, the higher your chances of living a fulfilled life. That task in your industry, organization, community or school that requires someone bold enough to go out on a limb to save the situation, should be an opportunity for you to raise your level of confidence and self-worth. When others shy away and give reasons why they cannot find a reason to do something, why you can and do it to prove a point to yourself.

Well, I hope you enjoyed this book, and it gave you plenty of value. It would be a great help if you left us a review telling us what you thought of the book.

www.ingramcontent.com/pod-product-compliance
Lightning Source LLC
Chambersburg PA
CBHW031118080526
44587CB00011B/1025